W0099553

Cambridge English

Starters 8

Answer Booklet

CAMBRIDGE
UNIVERSITY PRESS

University Printing House, Cambridge CB2 8BS, United Kingdom

Cambridge University Press is part of the University of Cambridge.

It furthers the University's mission by disseminating knowledge in the pursuit of
education, learning and research at the highest international levels of excellence.

www.cambridge.org
Information on this title: www.cambridge.org/9781107620049

© Cambridge University Press 2013

This publication is in copyright. Subject to statutory exception
and to the provisions of relevant collective licensing agreements,
no reproduction of any part may take place without the written
permission of Cambridge University Press.

First published 2013
6th printing 2015

Printed in China by Golden Cup Printing Co. Ltd

A catalogue record for this publication is available from the British Library

ISBN 978-1-107-62901-1 Student's Book
ISBN 978-1-107-62004-9 Answer Booklet
ISBN 978-1-107-63250-9 Audio CD

Cover design by Peter & Jan Simmonett
Produced by Kamae Design, Oxford

Cambridge University Press has no responsibility for the persistence or accuracy
of URLs for external or third-party internet websites referred to in this publication,
and does not guarantee that any content on such websites is, or will remain,
accurate or appropriate. Information regarding prices, travel timetables, and other
factual information given in this work is correct at the time of first printing but
Cambridge University Press does not guarantee the accuracy of such information
thereafter.

Contents

Introduction

The *Cambridge English: Young Learners* tests offer an elementary-level testing system (up to CEFR level A2) for learners of English between the ages of 7 and 12. The tests include three key levels of assessment: *Starters*, *Movers* and *Flyers*.

Starters is the lowest level in the system. Test instructions are very simple and consist only of words and structures specified in the syllabus.

The complete test lasts about 45 minutes and has the following components: Listening, Reading and Writing, and Speaking.

	length	number of parts	number of questions
Listening	approx. 20 minutes	4	20
Reading and Writing	20 minutes	5	25
Speaking	approx. 3–5 minutes	5	–

Candidates need a pen or pencil for the Reading and Writing paper, and coloured pens or pencils for the Listening paper. All answers are written on the question papers.

Listening

In general, the aim is to focus on the 'here and now' and to use language in meaningful contexts. In addition to multiple-choice and short-answer questions, candidates are asked to use coloured pencils to mark their responses to one of the tasks. There are four parts. Each part begins with a clear example.

part	main skill focus	input	expected response	number of questions
1	listening for words and prepositions	picture and dialogue	carry out instructions and position things correctly on a picture	5
2	listening for numbers and spelling	illustrated comprehension questions and dialogue	write numbers and names	5
3	listening for specific information of various kinds	3-option multiple-choice pictures and dialogues	tick correct box under picture	5
4	listening for words, colours and prepositions	picture and dialogue	carry out instructions; locate objects and colour correctly (range of colours is: black, blue, brown, green, grey, orange, pink, purple, red, yellow)	5

Reading and Writing

Again, the focus is on the 'here and now' and the use of language in meaningful contexts where possible. To complete the test, candidates need a single pen or pencil of any colour. There are five parts, each starting with a clear example.

part	main skill focus	input	expected response	number of questions
1	reading short sentences and recognising words	words, pictures and sentences	tick or cross to show if sentence is true or false	5
2	reading sentences about a picture and writing one-word answers	picture and sentences	write 'yes'/'no'	5
3	spelling of single words	pictures and sets of jumbled letters	write words	5
4	reading a text and copying words	cloze text, words and pictures	choose and copy missing words	5
5	reading questions about a picture story and writing one-word answers	story presented through three pictures and questions	write one-word answers to questions	5

Speaking

In the Speaking test, the candidate speaks with one examiner for about four minutes. The format of the test is explained in advance to the child in their native language, by a teacher or person familiar to them. This person then takes the child into the exam room and introduces them to the examiner.

Speaking ability is assessed according to various criteria, including comprehension, the ability to produce an appropriate response and pronunciation.

part	main skill focus	input	expected response
1	understanding and following spoken instructions	scene picture	point to the correct part of the picture
2	understanding and following spoken instructions	scene picture and eight small object cards	place the object cards on the scene picture as directed
3	understanding and answering spoken questions	scene picture	answer questions with short answers
4	understanding and answering spoken questions	three object cards	answer questions with short answers
5	understanding and responding to personal questions	no visual prompt	answer questions with short answers

Further information

The topics, structures, words and tasks upon which the *Cambridge English: Young Learners* tests are based are comprehensively described in the Handbook, so teachers or parents can know exactly what to expect.

Further information about the *Cambridge English: Young Learners* tests can be obtained from the Centre Exams Manager for Cambridge ESOL examinations in your area, or from:

University of Cambridge ESOL Examinations
1 Hills Road
Cambridge
CB1 2EU
United Kingdom

Telephone: +44 1223 553997
Fax: +44 1223 553621
Email: ESOLHelpdesk@CambridgeESOL.org
www.CambridgeESOL.org

Test 1 Answers

Listening

Part 1 (5 marks)
Lines should be drawn between:
1 the robot and in the armchair
2 the apple and between the children and the TV
3 the kite and next to the flowers
4 the T-shirt and on the floor, in front of the bookcase
5 the shoe and under the window

Part 2 (5 marks)
1 Read (correct spelling) 2 16/sixteen (children)
3 4/four (girls) 4 Tony (correct spelling)
5 Bill (correct spelling)

Part 3 (5 marks)
1 B 2 C 3 A 4 C 5 A

Part 4 (5 marks)
1 Colour the plane behind the helicopter – yellow
2 Colour the plane in the water – green
3 Colour the plane in the boy's hand – blue
4 Colour the plane in the tree – orange
5 Colour the plane between the babies, on the mat – red

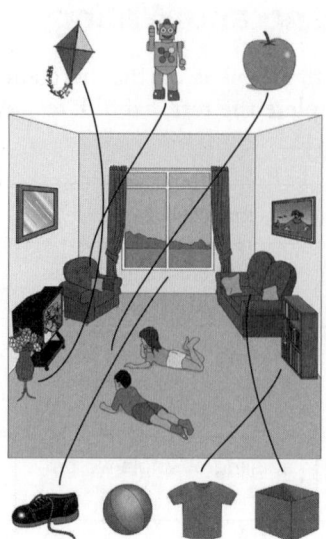

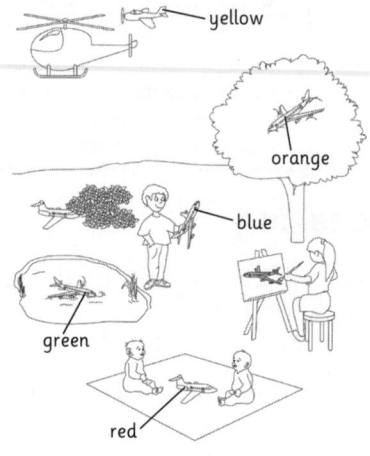

TRANSCRIPT   *Hello. This is the Cambridge Starters Practice Listening Test, Test 1.*

Part 1   *Look at Part 1. Now look at the picture. Listen and look. There is one example.*

[pause]

WOMAN: Put the box on the sofa.
MAN: Sorry? Where?
WOMAN: Put the box on the sofa.
MAN: Right.

[pause]

Can you see the line? This is an example.

Now you listen and draw lines.

[pause]

1

WOMAN: Now put the robot in the armchair.
MAN: Sorry, what?
WOMAN: Put the robot in the armchair.
MAN: Oh … yes! OK.

[pause]

2

WOMAN: OK. Now put the apple between the children and the TV.
MAN: Sorry? What?
WOMAN: The apple. Put it between the children and the TV.
MAN: OK.

[pause]

3

WOMAN: Now put the kite next to the flowers.
MAN: Pardon?
WOMAN: Put the kite next to the flowers.
MAN: Right.

[pause]

4

WOMAN: Can you see the T-shirt?
MAN: Yes.
WOMAN: Put the T-shirt on the floor in front of the bookcase.
MAN: OK. It's on the floor in front of the bookcase.

[pause]

5

WOMAN: Now the shoe. Put it under the window.
MAN: Sorry, where?
WOMAN: Put the shoe under the window.
MAN: OK.

Now listen to Part 1 again.

[The recording is repeated.]

[pause]

That is the end of Part 1.

[pause]

Part 2   *Look at the picture. Listen and write a name or a number.*

There are two examples.

[pause]

WOMAN: How old are you, Nick?
BOY: I'm seven.
WOMAN: Seven?
BOY: Yes, that's right.

[pause]

WOMAN: Where do you go to school, Nick?
BOY: Lime Tree School.
WOMAN: Is that L-I-M-E?
BOY: Yes, that's right.

[pause]

Can you see the answers?

Now you listen and write a name or a number.

[pause]

1

WOMAN: What's your teacher's name?
BOY: Miss Read.
WOMAN: How do you spell that?
BOY: R-E-A-D.
WOMAN: Oh, yes, I know her. I like her.

[pause]

2

BOY: We have very small classes at our school.
WOMAN: Oh, how many children are there in your class?
BOY: Sixteen.
WOMAN: Sixteen! That is a small class!

[pause]

3

WOMAN: And how many girls are there in your class?
BOY: There are four girls.
WOMAN: Four!
BOY: That's right.

[pause]

4

WOMAN: So, who sits next to you at school, Nick?
BOY: I sit next to Tony.
WOMAN: Is that T-O-N-Y?
BOY: Yes.
WOMAN: Oh, I like that name.

[pause]

5

WOMAN: Who do you play with at school?
BOY: I play with my friend, Bill.
WOMAN: Can you spell his name?
BOY: Yes, I can. It's B-I-L-L.

Now listen to Part 2 again.

[The recording is repeated.]

[pause]

That is the end of Part 2.

[pause]

Part 3   *Look at the pictures. Now listen and look.*

There is one example.

[pause]

What colour does Mum like?

GIRL: What can we buy for Mum's birthday? She wants a new bag, I know.
BOY: Good. We can buy a brown bag for her.
GIRL: No. She doesn't like brown. And she's got a black bag.
BOY: Well, we can buy a white bag, then. She likes that colour.

[pause]

Can you see the tick?

Now you listen and tick the box.

[pause]

1 What's Pat's favourite animal?

MAN: What's your favourite animal, Pat? Do you like elephants? Or crocodiles?
GIRL: Oh, no. I don't like those big animals.
MAN: Which animals do you like then?
GIRL: Mmm – monkeys!

[pause]

2 What's Sue doing?

MAN: Where's Sue? Is she watching TV?
WOMAN: No. She's in the kitchen.
MAN: Oh. Is she having her lunch?
WOMAN: No. She's reading a book.

[pause]

3 Which boy is Ben?

WOMAN: Do you go to school on the bus, Ben?

BOY: No, I don't.
WOMAN: Oh. Do you go on the train, then?
BOY: No. I ride my bike to school.

[pause]

4 What does May want for her
birthday?

MAN: What do you want for your birthday, May?
A new doll?
GIRL: No, thank you!
MAN: Oh. A new watch, then?
GIRL: No, thanks. Can I have a camera, please?

[pause]

5 Which is Sam's dad?

GIRL: Is that your dad, Sam? With the black
jacket?
BOY: No. My dad's wearing jeans and a shirt.
GIRL: Oh. Has he got glasses?
BOY: Yes, he has.

Now listen to Part 3 again.

[The recording is repeated.]

[pause]

That is the end of Part 3.

[pause]

Part 4   *Look at the picture. Listen and look.*

There is one example.

[pause]

MAN: Can you see the girl with the long hair?
She's painting a picture of a plane.
GIRL: Yes.
MAN: Well, colour that plane pink.
GIRL: Pardon?
MAN: The plane in the painting. Colour it pink.

[pause]

Can you see the pink plane in the
painting?

This is an example.

Now you listen and colour.

[pause]

1

MAN: There's a plane behind the helicopter.
GIRL: Yes, can I colour it?
MAN: Yes, colour it yellow.
GIRL: OK. The plane behind the helicopter, I'm
colouring it yellow.

[pause]

2

MAN: Find the plane in the water.
GIRL: Sorry?
MAN: The plane in the water. Colour it green.

GIRL: Green?
MAN: Yes.

[pause]

3

MAN: Can you see the boy? He's got a plane in
his hand.
GIRL: Yes.
MAN: Colour the plane in the boy's hand.
Colour it blue.
GIRL: OK. I'm colouring that plane blue.

[pause]

4

MAN: Now find the tree.
GIRL: Yes?
MAN: There's a plane in it. Colour it orange.
GIRL: Orange?
MAN: Yes, the plane in the tree.

[pause]

5

MAN: Look at the plane on the mat.
GIRL: Yes, it's between the two babies.
MAN: Yes. Colour that plane red.
GIRL: OK. There's a red plane between the
babies.
MAN: Yes, they love their toy plane!

Now listen to Part 4 again.

[The recording is repeated.]

[pause]

That is the end of the Starters Practice
Listening Test 1.

Reading and Writing

Part 1 (5 marks)

1 ✓   2 ✗   3 ✗   4 ✓   5 ✓

Part 2 (5 marks)

1 yes   2 no   3 no   4 no   5 yes

Part 3 (5 marks)

1 duck   2 frog   3 snake   4 hippo
5 crocodile

Part 4 (5 marks)

1 eggs   2 tail   3 legs   4 songs   5 cats

Part 5 (5 marks)

1 girl/child/daughter

2 (there are) three/3 (of them/monsters)

3 woman/lady/mum(my)/mother/mom(my)

4 (blue) trousers/jeans/pants

5 (red/pink) (small) bag/handbag

Speaking

Part	Examiner does this:	Examiner says this:	Minimum response expected from child:	Back-up questions:
	Usher brings candidate in.	Usher to examiner: **Hello. This is (child's name)*.** Examiner: **Hello, *. My name's** *Jane/Ms Smith.*	**Hello.**	
1	Points to **Scene** picture.	**Look at this. This is a garden. The children are in the garden with their dad.**		
	Points to the birds in **Scene** picture.	**Here are the birds. *, where's the cat? Where are the books?**	Points to items in the picture.	**Is this the cat? Are these the books?**
2	Points to **Object** cards.	**Now look at these. Which is the skirt/onion?**	Points to **Object** card.	**Is this the skirt/onion?** (pointing to skirt/onion)
		I'm putting the skirt/ onion in front of the door.		
		Now you put the skirt/ onion on the truck.	Puts **Object** card in place.	**Where's the truck? <u>On</u> the truck.**
		Which is the lamp?	Points to **Object** card.	**Is this the lamp?** (pointing to lamp)
		Put the lamp next to the flowers.	Puts **Object** card in place.	**Where are the flowers? <u>Next to</u> the flowers.**
		Which is the plane/chair?	Points to **Object** card.	**Is this the plane/chair?** (pointing to plane/chair)
		Put the plane/chair between the trees.	Puts **Object** card in place.	**Where are the trees? <u>Between</u> the trees.**
3	Removes **Object** cards and points to a frog in **Scene** picture.	**Now, *, what's this? What colour is it? How many frogs are there?**	**frog green five**	**Is it a frog? Is it red? Green? Are there four? Five?**
	Points to the man.	**What's the man doing?**	**painting**	**Is he painting?**
4	Puts **Scene** picture away and picks out three **Object** cards.			
4.1	Shows **ruler** card.	**What's this? Have you got a ruler? What colour is your/this ruler?**	**ruler** **yes/no** *pink*	**Is it a ruler?** **Is your/this ruler** *pink*?
4.2	Shows **grapes** card.	**What are these? Do you eat grapes? What's your favourite fruit?**	**grapes** **yes/no** *apple*	**Are they grapes?** **Do you like** *apples*?
4.3	Shows **baseball** card.	**What's this? Do you play baseball? What sport do you like?**	**baseball** **yes/no** *football*	**Is it baseball?** **Do you like** *football*?

* Remember to use the child's name throughout the test.

Part	Examiner does this:	Examiner says this:	Minimum response expected from child:	Back-up questions:
5	Puts away all cards.	**Now, *, where do you live?**	*(name of town or city)*	**Do you live in (*name of town or city*)?**
		Do you live in a flat / an apartment or a house?	*flat*	**Do you live in *a flat / an apartment*?**
		How many rooms are there in your flat/ apartment/house?	**6**	**Are there *six* rooms?**
		OK. Thank you, *.		
		Goodbye.	**Goodbye.**	

* Remember to use the child's name throughout the test.

Test 2 Answers

Listening

Part 1 (5 marks)

Lines should be drawn between:

1 the sock and on the mat
2 the radio and under the chair
3 the spider and on the hippo's foot
4 the frog and next to the shoe
5 the mirror and between the window and the picture

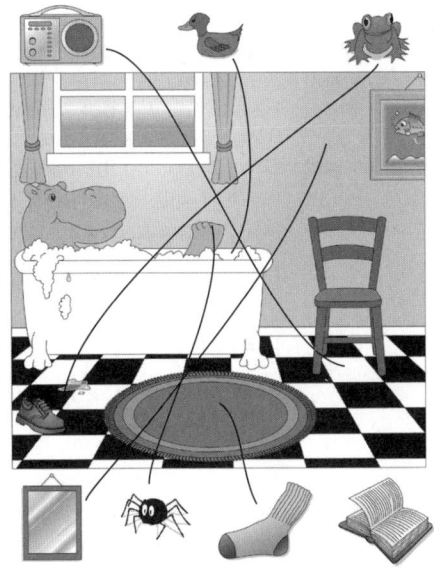

Part 2 (5 marks)

1 Gray (correct spelling)   2 5/five
3 Love (correct spelling)   4 9/nine
5 Ben (correct spelling)

Part 3 (5 marks)

1 A   2 B   3 C   4 B   5 C

Part 4 (5 marks)

1 Colour the head of the monster on the horse – pink
2 Colour the head of the monster wearing a dress – yellow
3 Colour the head of the monster kicking a football – red
4 Colour the head of the monster sleeping next to the flowers – purple
5 Colour the head of the flying monster – orange

(Accept if colouring overlaps beyond the head, but not if the whole monster is coloured.)

TRANSCRIPT   *Hello. This is the Cambridge Starters Practice Listening Test, Test 2.*

Part 1   *Look at Part 1. Now look at the picture. Listen and look. There is one example.*

[pause]

MAN: Can you see the duck?
WOMAN: Yes. Can I put it in the bath?
MAN: Yes, please put the duck in the bath.
WOMAN: OK.

[pause]

Can you see the line? This is an example.

Now you listen and draw lines.

[pause]

1

MAN: Now find the sock.
WOMAN: Yes …
MAN: And put it on the mat.
WOMAN: Right. The sock is on the mat now.

[pause]

2

WOMAN: And the radio?
MAN: The radio? Oh, yes. Please put it under the chair.
WOMAN: OK. I'm putting it under the chair now.
MAN: Thank you.

[pause]

3

WOMAN: I can see a spider. Where can I put it?
MAN: Please put the spider on the hippo's foot.
WOMAN: On the hippo's foot.
MAN: Yes, please.

[pause]

4

MAN: Here's a frog.
WOMAN: Yes, I can see it.
MAN: Please put it next to the shoe.
WOMAN: The frog is next to the shoe now.

[pause]

5

MAN: And can you find the mirror?
WOMAN: Yes, there it is.
MAN: Please can you put it between the window and the picture?
WOMAN: OK. I'm putting the mirror between the window and the picture.
Now listen to Part 1 again.

[The recording is repeated.]

[pause]

That is the end of Part 1.

[pause]

Part 2 *Look at the picture. Listen and write a name or a number.*

There are two examples.

[pause]

MAN: Hello, what's your name?
GIRL: It's Kim.
MAN: Oh, can you spell that?
GIRL: Yes, it's K-I-M.
MAN: Very good!

[pause]

MAN: And how old are you, Kim?
GIRL: I'm six now!
MAN: Pardon?
GIRL: I'm six.

[pause]

Can you see the answers?

Now you listen and write a name or a number.

[pause]

1

MAN: What school do you go to?
GIRL: I go to Gray School.
MAN: Can you spell Gray?
GIRL: Yes. G-R-A-Y.

[pause]

2

MAN: What class are you in?
GIRL: I'm in class five.
MAN: Five?
GIRL: Yes.

[pause]

3

GIRL: Our teacher is very good. I like her.
MAN: What's her name?
GIRL: Her name is Miss Love.

MAN: Is that L-O-V-E?
GIRL: Yes.

[pause]

4

MAN: And how many children are in your class?
GIRL: Nine.
MAN: Nine children? That's a small class.
GIRL: Yes, it is.

[pause]

5

MAN: And have you got a friend in your class?
GIRL: Yes, my friend Ben sits next to me.
MAN: Oh, that's nice. And do you write his name B-E-N?
GIRL: Yes, that's right.
Now listen to Part 2 again.

[The recording is repeated.]

[pause]

That is the end of Part 2.

[pause]

Part 3 *Look at the pictures. Now listen and look.*

There is one example.

[pause]

What's Bill doing?

MAN: Hello. Is Bill reading in his bedroom?
GIRL: No, he's in the street.
MAN: Oh, is he playing football?
GIRL: No, he's riding his bike.

[pause]

Can you see the tick?

Now you listen and tick the box.

[pause]

1 What does Tom want?

BOY: Mum, can I have a drink?
WOMAN: Yes. Do you want a drink of milk?
BOY: No, thanks.
WOMAN: Some lemonade then?
BOY: No. Can I have some pineapple juice, please?

[pause]

2 Which is Lucy?

MAN: Is that Lucy, the girl with the ice cream?
GIRL: No, that's Lucy there!
MAN: Oh, yes, the girl with the doll.
GIRL: I like her doll's hat.

[pause]

3 *What's for lunch?*

BOY: Mum, can I have a burger for lunch today?
WOMAN: Well, yes, but not with chips.
BOY: Can I have a tomato with it?
WOMAN: No … sorry. We've got some carrots in the kitchen. You can have those.
BOY: OK.

[pause]

4 *Where's Anna's pencil?*

GIRL: Dad! Dad! Where's my new pencil? Have you got it?
MAN: No. Look in your school bag.
GIRL: It isn't there, Dad, and it isn't on my desk.
MAN: Oh, look. There it is! Next to the phone.

[pause]

5 *Which picture does Nick like?*

BOY: Can I have a picture of an animal for my room, please?
WOMAN: Yes. Do you like this picture of an elephant?
BOY: No, and I don't like those giraffes.
WOMAN: And this picture of tigers? Do you like this?
BOY: Yes. It's great.

Now listen to Part 3 again.

[The recording is repeated.]

[pause]

That is the end of Part 3.

[pause]

Part 4   *Look at the picture. Listen and look.*

There is one example.

[pause]

WOMAN: Look at this picture.
BOY: Mmm. There are some monsters in a garden!
WOMAN: Now, can you see the monster with a dog?
BOY: Yes, I can see him. Can I colour his head blue?
WOMAN: Yes, please. The monster with the dog. Colour his head blue.

[pause]

Can you see the monster with the blue head? This is an example. Now you listen and colour.

[pause]

1

WOMAN: OK. There's a monster on a horse. Can you see him?
BOY: Yes, I can see him.
WOMAN: Can you colour that monster's head pink?
BOY: OK. The monster on the horse. His head is pink now.

[pause]

2

BOY: Look at that monster! She's wearing a dress!
WOMAN: Oh, yes! I like her dress.
BOY: Can I colour her head yellow?
WOMAN: Mmm. Yellow is a good colour for her head.

[pause]

3

BOY: What now?
WOMAN: Can you see the monster with the football?
BOY: Oh, yes. I can see him. He's kicking the football.
WOMAN: Colour his head red.
BOY: OK. His head is red now.

[pause]

4

BOY: Is that monster sleeping next to the flowers?
WOMAN: Yes.
BOY: Can I colour her head purple?
WOMAN: Yes, please. Colour the head of the monster next to the flowers purple.

[pause]

5

BOY: That monster is flying. Can I colour his head?
WOMAN: Yes. What colour?
BOY: My favourite colour is orange.
WOMAN: OK.
BOY: He's flying with an orange head now!

Now listen to Part 4 again.

[The recording is repeated.]

[pause]

That is the end of the Starters Practice Listening Test 2.

Reading and Writing

Part 1 (5 marks)

1 ✓   2 ✗   3 ✓   4 ✗   5 ✓

Part 2 (5 marks)

1 no   2 yes   3 no   4 no   5 yes

Part 3 (5 marks)

1 pear   2 orange   3 grapes   4 banana
5 coconut

Part 4 (5 marks)

1 eyes   2 mouth   3 legs   4 water   5 zoo

Part 5 (5 marks)

1 yellow   2 4/four   3 playground   4 boy
5 photo(graph)/picture

Speaking

Part	Examiner does this:	Examiner says this:	Minimum response expected from child:	Back-up questions:
	Usher brings candidate in.	Usher to examiner: **Hello. This is** *(child's name)**. Examiner: **Hello, *. My name's** *Jane/Ms Smith.*	**Hello.**	
1	Points to **Scene** picture.	**Look at this. This is a plane. The woman and children are walking to the plane.**		
	Points to the bird in **Scene** picture.	**Here's a black bird. *, where's the girl? Where are the cars?**	Points to items in the picture.	**Is this the girl? Are these the cars?**
2	Points to **Object** cards.	**Now look at these. Which is the camera?**	Points to **Object** card.	**Is this the camera?** (pointing to camera)
		I'm putting the camera on the motorbike.		
		Now you put the camera next to the boy.	Puts **Object** card in place.	**Where's the boy?** <u>Next to</u> **the boy.**
		Which is the sock/cat?	Points to **Object** card.	**Is this the sock/cat?** (pointing to sock/cat)
		Put the sock/cat in front of the man.	Puts **Object** card in place.	**Where is the man?** <u>In front of</u> **the man.**
		Which is the cake/ tomato?	Points to **Object** card.	**Is this the cake/tomato?** (pointing to cake/tomato)
		Put the cake/tomato between the flowers and the ball.	Puts **Object** card in place.	**Where are the flowers and the ball?** <u>Between</u> **the flowers and the ball.**
3	Removes **Object** cards and points to a monkey in **Scene** picture.	**Now, *, what's this? What colour is it? How many monkeys are there?**	monkey brown two	**Is it a monkey? Is it black? Brown? Are there three? Two?**
	Points to the dog.	**What's the dog doing?**	sleeping	**Is the dog sleeping?**
4	Puts **Scene** picture away and picks out three **Object** cards.			
4.1	Shows **jacket** card.	**What's this? Are you wearing a jacket?**	jacket yes/no	**Is it a jacket?**
		What colour is your/this jacket?	*blue*	**Is your/this jacket** *blue*?
4.2	Shows **fish** card.	**What's this? Have you got a fish? What's your favourite animal?**	fish yes/no *horse*	**Is it a fish?** **Do you like** *horses*?
4.3	Shows **orange juice** card.	**What's this? Do you like orange juice? What do you drink at breakfast?**	orange juice yes/no *milk*	**Is it orange juice?** **Do you drink** *milk*?

* Remember to use the child's name throughout the test.

Part	Examiner does this:	Examiner says this:	Minimum response expected from child:	Back-up questions:
5	Puts away all cards.	Now, *, how old are you?	9	Are you *nine*?
		Where do you learn English?	*(at) school*	Do you learn English *at school*?
		Is your school big or small?	*big*	Is your school *big*?
		OK. Thank you, *.		
		Goodbye.	Goodbye.	

* Remember to use the child's name throughout the test.

Test 3 Answers

Listening

Part 1 (5 marks)

Lines should be drawn between:

1 the carrot and in the box
2 the mouse and under the chair
3 the doll and on the bed
4 the frog and between the two shoes
5 the pineapple and next to the mirror

Part 2 (5 marks)

1 Cross (correct spelling)   2 4/four
3 Pat (correct spelling)   4 2/two
5 10/ten

Part 3 (5 marks)

1 C   2 A   3 B   4 A   5 A

Part 4 (5 marks)

1 Colour the woman's hat – purple
2 Colour the hat of the boy on the bike – orange
3 Colour the hat in the tree – blue
4 Colour the hat under the baby's feet – red
5 Colour the hat on the duck's head – yellow

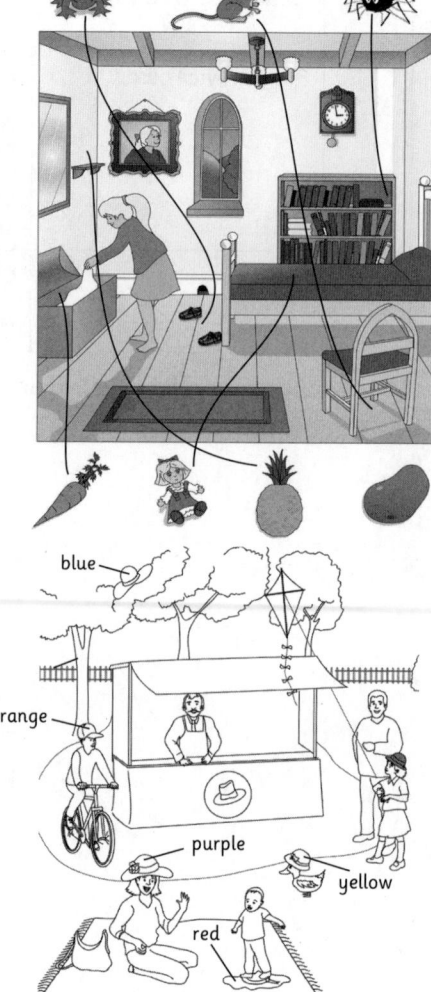

TRANSCRIPT   *Hello. This is the Cambridge Starters Practice Listening Test, Test 3.*

Part 1   *Look at Part 1. Now look at the picture. Listen and look. There is one example.*

[pause]

MAN: Can you see the spider?
WOMAN: Sorry, what?
MAN: The spider. Please put it in the bookcase.
WOMAN: OK. I'm putting it in the bookcase now.

[pause]

Can you see the line? This is an example. Now you listen and draw lines.

[pause]

1

MAN: Now the carrot. Can you put it in the box, please?
WOMAN: Pardon? Where can I put the carrot?
MAN: In the box, please.
WOMAN: Right.

[pause]

2

MAN: Now, put the mouse under the chair.
WOMAN: Sorry, put what under the chair?
MAN: The mouse, please.
WOMAN: OK.

[pause]

3

WOMAN: I can see a doll. Where can I put it?
MAN: Put the doll on the bed.
WOMAN: On the bed?
MAN: Yes, please.

[pause]

4

MAN: Now find the frog.
WOMAN: The frog. OK.
MAN: Put it between the two shoes.
WOMAN: Between the two shoes. OK, I'm doing that now.

[pause]

5

MAN: And can you find the pineapple?
WOMAN: Yes, I can see it.

MAN: Please can you put it next to the mirror?
WOMAN: OK, I'm putting the pineapple next to the mirror now.

Now listen to Part 1 again.

[The recording is repeated.]

[pause]

That is the end of Part 1.

[pause]

Part 2   *Look at the picture. Listen and write a name or a number.*

There are two examples.

[pause]

MAN: Hello, what's your name?
GIRL: It's Kim.
MAN: Oh, can you spell that?
GIRL: It's K-I-M.
MAN: Thank you.

[pause]

MAN: How many people live in your house?
GIRL: There are eight of us.
MAN: Eight?
GIRL: Yes. We're a big family.

[pause]

Can you see the answers?
Now you listen and write a name or a number.

[pause]

1

MAN: And where do you live, Kim?
GIRL: I live in Cross Street!
MAN: Is that C-R-O-double S?
GIRL: That's right.

[pause]

2

MAN: And what number is your house?
GIRL: It's number four.
MAN: Sorry, what number?
GIRL: Four.
MAN: Thank you.

[pause]

3

GIRL: My grandma lives with us.
MAN: Oh, what's her name?
GIRL: Grandma? It's Pat.
MAN: Can you spell that?
GIRL: Yes, it's P-A-T.

[pause]

4

MAN: And do you have a brother?
GIRL: I've got two brothers.
MAN: Two?
GIRL: Yes. That's right.

[pause]

5

GIRL: It's my big brother's birthday today.
MAN: Oh? How old is he?
GIRL: He's ten today!
MAN: Ten?
GIRL: Yes, that's right. And I love my brother! He's great!

Now listen to Part 2 again.

[The recording is repeated.]

[pause]

That is the end of Part 2.

[pause]

Part 3   *Look at the pictures. Now listen and look. There is one example.*

[pause]

What's Bill's favourite fruit?

MAN: Mmm. This mango is nice. What fruit do you like, Bill?
BOY: Well, I don't like mangoes. And I don't like apples!
MAN: Grapes are my favourite.
BOY: Me too!

[pause]

Can you see the tick?

Now you listen and tick the box.

[pause]

1 Which bag can May have?

GIRL: Mum, can I have a new bag? This one's got flowers on it and I don't like it.
WOMAN: Yes, May. You can choose.
GIRL: Wow! Can I have this one?
WOMAN: No, May. It's too small. Have this big bag with a cow on it.

[pause]

2 What is Grandad's favourite game?

BOY: Do you like football, Grandad?
MAN: It's OK, but I love basketball.
BOY: And baseball – do you like that?
MAN: No, I don't.

[pause]

3 What can the boy have for lunch today?

BOY: Mum, what can I have for lunch today? Sausages?
WOMAN: No. You can have fish.
BOY: OK, but can I have chips with it?
WOMAN: No, you can have rice with it.

[pause]

4 Where's Ben going?

MAN: Hello, Ben. Are you going to school?
BOY: No, there are no lessons today. I'm walking to my friend's house.
MAN: Oh! Does he live next to the park?
BOY: No. He lives next to the zoo.

[pause]

5 What's Anna drawing?

MAN: What are you drawing, Anna? Is it a hippo?
GIRL: No, Dad! Try again.
MAN: Is it an elephant?
GIRL: No, look, it's a horse.

Now listen to Part 3 again.

[The recording is repeated.]

[pause]

That is the end of Part 3.

[pause]

Part 4 *Look at the picture. Listen and look.*

There is one example.

[pause]

WOMAN: Look at the picture. Can you see the girl with a kite?
BOY: Yes. Can I colour her hat?
WOMAN: Yes. Colour it green.
BOY: Pardon?
WOMAN: The girl with the kite. Make her hat green.

[pause]

Can you see the green hat? This is an example. Now you listen and colour.

[pause]

1

BOY: And the woman's wearing a hat too.
WOMAN: Oh, yes. Colour that hat purple.
BOY: OK. I'm colouring the woman's hat purple now.
WOMAN: Good.

[pause]

2

WOMAN: Can you see the boy on the bike? He's wearing a hat. Colour his hat orange.
BOY: Orange? That's a nice colour!
WOMAN: Yes, and the boy on the bike likes it.

[pause]

3

BOY: And why is there a hat in the tree?
WOMAN: I don't know. Would you like to colour it?
BOY: OK.
WOMAN: Colour it blue.
BOY: Right. The hat in the tree is blue now.

[pause]

4

BOY: Is that baby standing on a hat?
WOMAN: Yes. That's not very nice!
BOY: Can I colour that hat?
WOMAN: Yes, please. Colour the hat under the baby's feet, red.
BOY: OK. I'm doing it red now.

[pause]

5

BOY: Look at the duck! It's got a big hat on its head!
WOMAN: Yes.
BOY: Can I make its hat yellow? That's my favourite colour.
WOMAN: Yes, please. Colour the hat on the duck's head, yellow.

Now listen to Part 4 again.

[The recording is repeated.]

[pause]

That is the end of the Starters Practice Listening Test 3.

Reading and Writing

Part 1 (5 marks)

1 ✗   2 ✓   3 ✗   4 ✓   5 ✗

Part 2 (5 marks)

1 no   2 yes   3 no   4 yes   5 yes

Part 3 (5 marks)

1 leg   2 eye   3 face   4 hair   5 mouth

Part 4 (5 marks)

1 buses   2 flats   3 shop   4 school
5 dogs

Part 5 (5 marks)

1 (foot)ball
2 sleeping
3 boys/children/kids/grandsons/grandchildren/ grandkids/brothers
4 bird(s)
5 Grandpa/Grandfather/Gran(d)dad/man

Speaking

Part	Examiner does this:	Examiner says this:	Minimum response expected from child:	Back-up questions:
	Usher brings candidate in.	Usher to examiner: **Hello. This is (child's name)*.**		
		Examiner: **Hello, *. My name's** *Jane/Ms Smith.*	**Hello.**	
1	Points to **Scene** picture.	**Look at this. This is a living room. The girl is getting her toys.**		
	Points to the window in **Scene** picture.	**Here's the window. *, where's the lamp? Where are the cars?**	Points to items in the picture.	**Is this the lamp? Are these the cars?**
2	Points to **Object** cards.	**Now look at these. Which is the hat?**	Points to **Object** card.	**Is this the hat?** (pointing to hat)
		I'm putting the hat on the bookcase.		
		Now you put the hat behind the boy.	Puts **Object** card in place.	**Where's the boy?** <u>Behind</u> **the boy.**
		Which is the camera/ radio?	Points to **Object** card.	**Is this the camera/radio?** (pointing to camera/radio)
		Put the camera/radio under the big table.	Puts **Object** card in place.	**Where's the big table?** <u>Under</u> **the big table.**
		Which is the fish/ice cream?	Points to **Object** card.	**Is this the fish/ice cream?** (pointing to fish/ice cream)
		Put the fish/ice cream between the sofa and the door.	Puts **Object** card in place.	**Where are the sofa and the door?** <u>Between</u> **the sofa and the door.**
3	Removes **Object** cards and points to the black cat in **Scene** picture.	**Now, *, what's this? What colour is it? How many cats are there?**	**cat** **black** **three**	**Is it a cat? Is it white? Black? Are there two? Three?**
	Points to the woman.	**What's the woman doing?**	**phoning/talking**	**Is the woman phoning?**

* Remember to use the child's name throughout the test.

Part	Examiner does this:	Examiner says this:	Minimum response expected from child:	Back-up questions:
4	Puts **Scene** picture away and picks out three **Object** cards.			
4.1	Shows **chips/fries** card.	What are these? Do you eat chips/fries? What do you eat for dinner?	chips/fries yes/no *chicken*	Are they chips/fries? Do you eat *chicken* for dinner?
4.2	Shows **eyes** card.	What are these? Do you wear glasses? What colour are your eyes?	eyes yes/no *green*	Are they eyes? Are your eyes *green*?
4.3	Shows **TV** card.	What's this? Do you like watching TV/ television? How many TVs/ televisions are there in your house/flat/ apartment?	TV/television yes/no *2*	Is it a TV/television? Are there *two* TVs/ televisions in your house/flat/apartment?
5	Puts away all cards.	Now, *, how old are you? What's your mother's name? Is your mother's hair long or short?	*10* *Anna* *long*	Are you *10*? Is your mother's name *Anna*? Is your mother's hair *long*?
		OK. Thank you, *. Goodbye.	 Goodbye.	

* Remember to use the child's name throughout the test.

STARTERS THEMATIC VOCABULARY LIST

For ease of reference, vocabulary is arranged in semantic groups or themes. Some words appear under more than one heading.

In addition to the topics, notions and concepts listed for the syllabus, the following categories appear:

- useful words and expressions
- adjectives
- determiners
- adverbs
- prepositions
- conjunctions
- pronouns
- verbs
- modals
- question words
- names

ANIMALS

animal
bird
cat
chicken
cow
crocodile
dog
duck
elephant
fish (s & pl)
frog
giraffe
goat
hippo
horse
lizard
monkey
mouse/mice
sheep (s & pl)
snake
spider
tail
tiger
zoo

THE BODY & FACE

arm
body
ear
eye
face
foot/feet
hair
hand
head
leg
mouth
nose
smile

CLOTHES

bag
clothes
dress
glasses
handbag
hat
jacket
jeans
shirt
shoe
skirt
sock
trousers
T-shirt
watch
wear

COLOURS

black
blue
brown
colour
green
grey (US gray)
orange
pink
purple
red
white
yellow

FAMILY & FRIENDS

baby
boy
brother
child/children
cousin
dad(dy)
family
father
friend
girl
grandfather
grandma
grandmother
grandpa
live
man/men
Miss
mother
Mr
Mrs
mum(my) (US mom(my))
old
person/people
sister
their
them
they
us
we
woman/women
you
young
your

FOOD & DRINK

apple
banana
bean
bread
breakfast
burger
cake
candy (UK sweet(s))
carrot
chicken
chips (US fries)
chocolate

coconut
dinner
drink (n & v)
eat
egg
fish
food
fries (UK chips)
fruit
grape
ice cream
juice
lemon
lemonade
lime
lunch
mango
meat
milk
onion
orange
pea
pear
pineapple
potato
rice
sausage
supper
sweet(s) (US candy)
tomato
water
watermelon

THE HOME

apartment (UK flat)
armchair
bath
bathroom
bed
bedroom
bookcase
box
camera
chair
clock
computer
cupboard
desk
dining room
doll
door
flat (US apartment)
floor
flower
garden
hall
home
house
kitchen
lamp
living room
mat
mirror

painting
phone
picture
radio
room
sleep
sofa
table
television/TV
toy
tree
wall
watch
window

NUMBERS

Cardinals: 1–20

PLACES & DIRECTIONS

behind
between
bookshop
here
in
in front of
next to
on
park
shop (US store)
store (UK shop)
street
there
under
zoo

SCHOOL

alphabet
answer
ask
board
book
bookcase
class
classroom
close
colour
computer
correct
cross
cupboard
desk
door
draw(ing)
English
eraser (UK rubber)
example
find
floor
keyboard (computer)
know
learn
lesson

letter (as in alphabet)
line
listen (to)
look
mouse (computer)
music
name
number
open
page
part
pen
pencil
picture
playground
question
read
right (as in correct)
rubber (US eraser)
ruler
school
sentence
sit
spell
stand (up)
story
teacher
tell
test (n & v)
tick (n & v)
understand
wall
window
word
write

SPORTS & LEISURE

badminton
ball
baseball
basketball
beach
bike
boat
book
bounce
camera
catch
doll
draw(ing)
drive (v)
enjoy
favourite
fish(ing)
fly
football (US soccer)
game
guitar
hit
hobby
hockey
jump
kick (v)

kite
listen (to)
music
paint(ing)
photo
piano
picture
play (with)
radio
read
ride (v)
run
sing
soccer (UK football)
song
sport
story
swim (v)
table tennis
take a photo/picture
television/TV
tennis
throw
toy
walk (v)
watch

TIME

afternoon
birthday
clock
day
end
evening
morning
night
today
watch
year

TOYS

alien
ball
balloon
baseball
basketball
bike
boat
car
doll
football
game
helicopter
kite
lorry (US truck)
monster
plane
robot
toy
train
truck (UK lorry)

TRANSPORT

bike
boat
bus
car
drive (v)
fly (v)
go
helicopter
lorry (US truck)
motorbike
plane
ride (v)
run
swim
train
truck (UK lorry)

WEATHER

sun

WORK

teacher

THE WORLD AROUND US

beach
sand
sea
shell
street
sun
tree
water

USEFUL WORDS & EXPRESSIONS

bye (-bye)
goodbye
hello
I don't know
no
oh
oh dear
OK
pardon
please
right
so
sorry
thank you
thanks
then
well
well done
wow!
yes

ADJECTIVES

angry
beautiful

big
clean
closed
correct
dirty
double
English
favourite
funny
good
great
happy
her
his
its
long
my
new
nice
OK
old
open
our
right (correct)
sad
short
small
sorry
their
ugly
young
your

DETERMINERS

a/an
a lot of
lots of
many
no
one
some
that
the
these
this
those

ADVERBS

a lot
again
here
home
lots
no
not
now
really
there
today
too
very
yes

PREPOSITIONS

about
at (prep of place)
behind
between
for
from
in (prep of place)
in front of
like
next to
of
on (prep of place)
to
under
with

CONJUNCTIONS

and
but
or

PRONOUNS

a lot
he
her
hers
him
his
I
it
its
lots
me
mine
one
ours
she
that
theirs
them
these
they
this
those
us
we
you
yours

VERBS

Irregular:
be
catch (a ball)
choose
come
do
draw
drink
drive
eat

find
fly
get
give
go
have
have (got)
hit
hold
know
learn
let's
make
put
read
ride
run
say
see
sing
sit (down)
sleep
spell
stand (up)
swim
take (a photo)
tell
throw
understand
wear
write

Regular:
add
answer
ask
bounce
clean
close
colour
complete
cross
enjoy
jump
kick
learn
like
listen (to)
live
look
look at
love
open
paint
phone
pick up
play (with)
point
show
smile
start
stop
talk

test
tick
try
walk
want
watch
wave

MODALS

can/cannot/can't

QUESTION WORDS

how
how many
how old
what
where
which
who
whose

NAMES

Alex
Ann
Anna
Ben
Bill
Dan
Grace
Jill
Kim
Lucy
May
Nick
Pat
Sam
Sue
Tom
Tony